W9-CQH-237

The Zen of
Genealogy

The Zen of Genealogy

LOIS JESEK

The Lighter Side of Genealogy

By BETH MALTBIE UYEHARA

Design and Illustrations by Lois Jesek

HERITAGE BOOKS, INC.

Copyright 2002
Beth Maltbie Uyehara

Design and Illustrations by Lois Jesek

Published 2002 by
HERITAGE BOOKS, INC.
1540E Pointer Ridge Place, Bowie, Maryland 20716
1-800-398-7709
www.heritagebooks.com

ISBN 0-7884-2272-3

A Complete Catalog Listing Hundreds of Titles
On History, Genealogy, and Americana
Available Free Upon Request

To Tak

Thank you

A number of people have helped us put this little book together, and it's hardly possible to thank them enough. But I'll try.

The extraordinary talents of the illustrator and designer, Lois Jesek, are on display from cover to cover, but beyond her many skills, she has been a true joy to collaborate with. She has made this such fun! Her charming drawings (especially the ebullient "Matilda" lead character) capture the spirit of the "Worm's Eye View" columns perfectly and add immeasurably to the final product. Thanks, fellow Sagittarian.

I'd also like to thank another dear friend and former co-worker, Terri Niccum, who has lent her considerable editing and proofreading skills to try to save me from myself (which is not always an easy task).

Profuse thanks go also to John Jesek, who has provided invaluable technical advice, moral support and encouragement all along, and to Paul Uyehara, who has borne the brunt of all of this for months now, and whose support and encouragement never falters.

There's no way to thank Myra Vanderpool Gormley enough for introducing me to genealogy in the first

Acknowledgments

place, and fitting me with my training wheels (which I'm still wearing). It's been a blast and a half, Myra . . . and here's another fine mess you got me into.

A very special thanks goes also to Julie Case, who, as "co-editor at fault" with Myra, gave me the opportunity to be published in the online genealogy magazine, "Missing Links." (And who taught me how to spell Monkees.) Several of the "Worms Eye View" columns in this book first appeared in "Missing Links," and I appreciate Julie's generosity in allowing them to be republished here.

The little limerick, "The Enron Ancestor," on page 75, first appeared in "The Searcher," the publication of the Southern California Genealogical Society, and I thank them for permission to reprint it here.

Finally, I can't possibly thank by name all the people who have responded to my columns in "Missing Links" by sending me such warm and encouraging e-mails — but your kind and positive feedback is why I keep trying to write these silly things. And a very special thank you — and blame — goes to those of you who wrote, "Why don't you put these together into a book?"

TABLE OF CONTENTS

The Zen of
Genealogy

. . . meditation

The Zen of Genealogy

I've been doing yoga now for about ten years, and genealogy for six, and suddenly, both are trendy. It's the first time in my life I've ever been ahead of the curve. (When Madonna finally discovers genealogy, we'll be so inundated with hype that we'll all be sick of family history within a week.)

A disclaimer: When I say that I have been doing yoga for ten years, this is not to imply that I can, as yet, actually touch my toes. But my yoga teacher has explained to me that yoga works on many levels, and that – on a spiritual level – I can probably touch my spiritual toes. As to the physical level – or the "gross body," as we yoginis put it – it may take a couple more lifetimes for me to get my actual fingers past my actual knees. Some bodies are grosser than others.

But, that aside, the point is that we've got two humongous trends going on here. Why not combine them into one really stupid fad? (Think pet rocks and mood rings.)

Here are some simple yogealogy exercises (gen-kriyas) to get you started. All mantras are to be repeated for the duration of the exercise, except when noted otherwise.

Rock Pose

Posture: Sit in a silent, darkened room in front of a microfilm reader, peering intently at pale, blurry handwriting. (Your eyes may soon glaze over. Don't worry. This is normal.)

Lean forward tensely at an uncomfortable angle. Hold this position for eight hours.

Mudra /Action: While maintaining the posture, raise your right hand in front of you at a 45-degree angle from your body, and make slow, circular, cranking motions until you lose all feeling in your right arm.

Mantra: (Repeat silently) Please, please, please, please, please, please.

Plow Pose

Posture: Position a tall stack of index books on a library table. Crouch in front of the stack.

Mudra /Action: Make a fist of your left hand, with the index finger extended. Slowly run the extended finger down page after page of the first book. Close book, set aside and repeat with next book. Plow through the whole stack, then drag the stack in front of you again and repeat. Continue plowing until library closes.

Mantra: (Repeat silently) Where? Where? Where? Where? Where? Where?

Crow Pose

Posture: Form two fists and thrust both arms upward. Throw back your head, grin maniacally, squeeze your eyes shut. This exercise can be performed either seated or standing; for maximum effect, begin in a seated position with the upward arm thrust, then leap suddenly to your feet, knocking over your chair behind you.

Mudra /Action: From time to time, drop your head to your chest, bend your right arm and pump your fist vigorously. Variation: Perform clog dance around fallen chair.

Mantra: (Shout exultantly) Yesssss! Yesssss! Yesssss! Yesssss! I found it! Hahahahahahahahah.

Continue until ejected from the premises.

Tree Pose

Posture: (Best done in the back of a crowded research seminar.) Obtain an eight-pound syllabus, two bulky notebooks and three grocery sacks full of newly purchased, very thick, very heavy, hardcover books. Clutch these items to your chest with both arms. Simultaneously, dangle a heavy purse from your left shoulder and a heavy tote bag from your right shoulder. (Men: Instead of a purse, obtain a second tote bag and fill with rocks.) Stand erect stretching neck as high as possible to see over people standing in front of you.

Mudra /Action: (Hiss through clenched teeth): What'd he say? What'd he say? What'd he say?

Downward Dog

Posture: (Must be done in a cemetery.) Place yourself squarely in front of a weathered tombstone, facing the stone. With your feet flat on the ground, lean forward until your hands are also resting on the ground. Your body will form an isosceles triangle, with your rear end at the apex. Raise you head and squint at the tombstone.

Mudra /Action: Balancing carefully, raise your right

Downward dog

arm and run your fingertips very lightly over the surface of the stone, attempting to decipher it. Hold your breath, and continue for one minute.

Mantra: (At end of the minute, exclaim once, explosively) Piffle!

Move to the next tombstone.

Repeat until sunset.

Corpse Pose

Posture: (Can be done anywhere, but is most frequently performed on the floor in the privacy of one's home.) To assume posture, collapse flat on your back, legs outstretched, arms at side, hands upturned helplessly. Roll your eyes up to focus on a point in the middle of your forehead.

Mudra /Action: Alternately twitch your left eyelid and right shoulder. Repeat for five minutes, then slowly and rhythmically begin banging the back of your head against the floor. Bang for five minutes. Alternate twitching and banging until someone throws a bucket of cold water in your face.

Mantra: (In a loud, plaintive wail during the banging phase) Why didn't I ask Grandma when I had the chance?! Why? WHY?!?

Mastering these few, simple yogealogy gen-kriyas, will mean that you, too, will soon be on the cutting edge of cool, the envy of hip-hop hype-meisters everywhere.

The Worm's Eye View

. . . and your g-g-g-grandfather

How to Win
Friends and Fascinate
Your Relatives

enealogy offers many attractions that continue to lure new converts to the field, such as the thrill of wandering, lost, in an abandoned graveyard as night falls and wolves howl in the gloaming . . .

Or, the delight of discovering – in faded ink and really bad handwriting – that your g-grandfather was either a "Prince Somebody," or a "Prime Suspect" or a "Pineapple Soufflé" . . .

Or the opportunity to spend every hard-earned vacation minute in a musty library, squinting at medieval parish records written in a long-forgotten Ukrainian dialect that has yet to be decoded.

Talk about a fascinating hobby! How could stamp collecting, high-stakes poker or sky diving compare to these madcap genealogical adventures? Yet, oddly enough, one of the most rewarding aspects of this pastime is often overlooked, even by its most avid practitioners.

To my mind, the ultimate benefit of genealogical

research is that nothing makes you more popular with your relatives than sharing your genealogy findings. You'll be the star of every holiday gathering when you wheel in your latest research on a forklift, and unpack your tape recorder, digital camera, lie detector and DNA kit on your cousin's kitchen table.

Relatives who never noticed you before will snap to attention when you shove a tape recorder in the face of sweet old Auntie Maude, and say, "According to my records, Auntie M., you were born in 1927, not 1935 as you claimed on your 1956 marriage license. This makes you six years older than your husband, not two years younger. Also, I noticed that your nine-pound, seven-ounce first child was born only two months after your marriage. What's the story on that? Fill us in."

Once her good-natured chuckles subside and her face resumes its normal flesh color, she'll thank you for setting the record straight – and will probably rush right home to alter her will with you in mind.

Catching out your relatives in their little white lies, demolishing long-told family legends about royal antecedents, dredging up embarrassing facts concerning the real reasons your immigrant ancestors left the old country so abruptly, revealing long-suppressed family secrets (and sometimes, in an excess of enthusiasm, posting them to the Internet) and deflating colorful family anecdotes – there is no better way to endear yourself to your relatives than by investigating the family's actual, honest-to-gosh past, and then telling the world about it. It's important to never flinch from the sordid facts you uncover, or hesitate at the need to embellish the already-lurid details for the sake of a better story line.

If your relatives are like mine, they may be shy about showing you just how much they appreciate your efforts to debunk family myths. Don't let that slow you down. The mark of a good genealogist is the ability to pursue the truth, even when cornered by an incensed mob of cousins brandishing pitchforks and hurling rocks and insults in your direction.

But, what if, despite your slick PowerPoint presentations and 20-generation fan charts, your family remains unimpressed? Or even worse, bored and hostile? Alas, some families are more genealogy-resistant than others.

In this unlikely event, just keep reminding them how fascinating it all is. Sprinkle your narration about your latest finds with such comments as, "This next part is especially fascinating." "Wow! Isn't this just too fascinating for words?" "Hoo boy, now we're getting to the really fascinating part." By including these subtle reminders in your presentations, your genealogy holdouts can quickly be brought into the fold.

It's important that you clamp down on any hostility to genealogy early in your research career; otherwise, like a lone fireman facing a raging brush fire, you may never get it contained. Some of the subtle signs indicating that your relatives' enthusiasm for your research is flagging are:

- their eyes glaze over and slowly roll up under their eyelids when you start talking;

- their heads fall back against the couch, jaws sagging open;

- you hear snoring sounds and observe

trickles of drool running down their chins;

- your cousins edge out of the room at your first mention of the word "fascinating";

- your siblings "accidentally" set fire to your family group sheets and/or your hair;

- your parents slash your tires and petition the court to change their surname.

Should you detect any of these subtle signs of ennui or resistance, your best bet is to just talk louder. Enunciate very carefully. Shove your face close to the person you're talking to, and grab his lapels. You have my permission to shout, if necessary, to bring their attention back from the Super Bowl to your analysis of the distribution of the RH-negative blood factor among your maternal second cousins.

. . . and our g-g-g-grandfather was banished from the Old Country

The secret to genealogy, after all, is perseverance. If you talk about your research long enough, and loud enough, in enough excruciating detail, to enough bored or scandalized relatives, some of them are bound to catch the genealogy bug, too. It could happen . . . maybe not in this lifetime (and certainly not in my family), but, it might happen in yours.

Just keep reminding them that not only is this stuff really, really fascinating, but you're only doing it for their sake.

Let me know if this works.

<(oo)>

and married g-g-g-grandmother Hilda Mae, who had eight kids.

Go for the gold!

Go
for the Gold!

When it was announced that the 2002 Winter Olympics had been awarded to Salt Lake City, I thought, "Aha! At last, genealogy is being recognized as an Olympic sport."

Why else would they have chosen the home of that world-class sporting venue, the Family History Library? And, what better activity could they find than genealogy to demonstrate the thrill of victory, the agony of defeat, the scandal of bad judgment calls, and the pathos of years spent in dogged pursuit of obscure and unremunerated goals?

It was, therefore, a surprise to learn that Salt Lake City had been chosen because of its mountains, ski resorts, fine powder snow, and things of that ilk.

Who cares about any of that, when there's one of the world's great genealogical libraries at hand? Like many of you, I'm sure, I watched the Olympics on TV in growing dismay as nary a genealogist hove into view. What a waste of Salt Lake City's finest resource the 2002 games proved to be.

To rectify that omission, I am awarding my own gold medals for the Family History Library's outstanding genealogical performances. Here are my choices for the fastest, longest and strongest performances in the field. If you disagree with my picks, I will only say in my defense that I am 1/32 French, and this otherwise-proud heritage occasionally causes lapses in judgment.

Here are my categories in competitive genealogy:

Longest Research Marathon Without a Potty Break

The individual world record was established in 1992 by a woman from Alaska whose iron constitution (not to mention bladder) allowed her to research for twelve hours continuously, without once leaving her seat at the microfilm reader.

We salute her!

The Four-Floor Scramble

In 1975, a gentleman from St. Louis established a world record that still stands: He single-handedly kept seats warm and/or microfilm readers humming for ten hours straight on four separate floors.

He accomplished this by combining elevators and stairs, hurling himself downward from the second floor, banking himself off an angle of the staircase and into a corner pocket of the book stacks on the first floor, then leaping up minutes later to careen through the lobby to the elevators to B1 and B2, where his respective microfilm readers were still smoking from his last visit.

All hail the victor!

The One-Man Lunge

This was one of the closest contests in competitive

genealogical history. The photo finish showed that the winner was a young man from Memphis, who lunged ahead of an elderly lady from Boston to reach the only unoccupied copier on the first floor.

There was some concern about his tactics – the Canadian judge felt that kicking the lady's cane from her hand had been unsporting – but in the end the young man was awarded the gold.

Cheers and huzzahs!

The Downhill Fizzle

The world-record deflation of a carefully worked-out pedigree was accomplished in five seconds flat by a researcher from Minneapolis, when she suddenly realized that her ancestor John Smith, born in 1802, could not possibly be the same John Smith who had fought heroically in the Revolutionary War (1774-1783) whom, alas, she had been researching for 27 years.

There, but for the grace of God go we all!

Fastest Lunch Break

(Ahem), not to be immodest, but, I believe I hold this record, which I established in 1998, when I hid an open bag of crackers behind the vending machine in the lunch room, allowing me, a few hours later, to gallop in, push the more leisurely diners aside, cram my mouth full of crackers and be back in my seat hard at work before the last crumb disappeared down my gullet.

Hip, hip hurrah, if I do say so myself!

The Turnstile Hurdle

In her eagerness to get started on her research in the few days allotted for that purpose, a genealogist from Australia leaped and cleared the entry turnstile by a good six inches, only to be nailed in midair by a Mormon missionary's flawlessly executed triple-axel flying tackle. This was a double gold-medal-winning performance by both the researcher and the aging missionary, and has permanently inscribed both their names in the record book.

Let's hear it for two good sports!

The Combined: Greatest Leap of Faith/ Skating on Thin Ice Short Form

Working at her laptop, a researcher from Atlanta found an Internet home page that mentioned an ancestor with a name something like the one she was researching. Hesitating only a moment to glance furtively around, the woman boldly cut-and-pasted the information into her own research notes, and "saved" the information for a perfect landing.

You go, girl!

Of course these are only the winter genealogy competitions. Winners of such summer events as clean-and-jerk weight lifting; Serb, Czech and Pole vaulting; and diving off the deep end will be covered in a separate account.

And so, as the setting sun casts a golden glow over the Wasatch Range and the trumpets blare the Olympic theme for the last time across the deserted ski slopes, we bid fond farewell to Salt Lake City – city of mountains, powder snow, courage, inspiration, endurance, faith, hope and genealogy.

EZ Duz It

Hi . . . My name is Beth. M.U., and I'm a geneaholic. My story's not a pretty one. I am sharing it here in the hope that it may help others avoid my pitiful fate. If you, too, are addicted to genealogy, I want you to know that you are not alone. There are thousands of us worldwide struggling in the daily battle against this cunning, baffling and powerful addiction.

There was something "different" about me from the get-go. Looking back, the signs were there for all to see. Even as a child, when relatives threw old Daguerreotypes in the trash, I would fish around among the coffee grounds and egg shells and pull them out. When old letters or diaries were discovered in musty trunks, I stayed up all night reading them. Obits, report cards, discharge papers, photos of unknown people: I hoarded them all.

I didn't care what kind of document it was, or who it concerned – if it was remotely connected to "family," I had to have it.

I'm making no excuses. I had a good upbringing. Genealogy certainly doesn't run in my family – I come from a long line of people who could take their ancestors or leave them alone. Yes, there were rumors of an aunt on my father's side who "did a little research on weekends," but she covered her tracks well, and I have never been able to prove for certain that she was a geneaholic.

Aside from that one suspect, my relatives were all what we call "social genealogists." For them, a colorful fore-bear or two were good for party conversations, to be chuckled over at family gatherings, and that was it.

Not me. Right from the beginning, I was out of control. I could never stop with just one or two ancestors. Every ancestor I found triggered an insatiable craving in me for two more, and four more after that, and eight more after that.

I could not stop once I got started.

Eventually, genealogy took over my life. Bouts of com-pulsive research would leave me babbling incoherently, slumped exhausted, sometimes barely conscious, at a microfilm reader in some darkened room, surrounded by other addicts satisfying their own shameful cravings for genealogical kicks.

Many are the times I've been thrown out of a library at closing time, kicking and screaming, begging for just five minutes more, just "one more ancestor for the road." It was humiliating.

As the years went by, things went from bad to worse. It was an endless downward spiral. I found myself sneaking from library to library in distant parts of town, even in other cities and states, searching for the ultimate high – that mysterious immigrant ancestor, whose identity would make everything fall into place.

I hit bottom one hot August day in a cemetery in a far-off state. How I got there doesn't matter. Let's just say that after much research, I had located the grave of an ancestor who – according to family legend – had died in some kind of accident.

As I stared at the weathered, old tombstone, wondering how I could find out how he had died, the thought occurred to me: "I could dig him up and see." Immediately, I recoiled, aghast.

Eeeeuuuu, I cried, yuk! That's gross.

That's when I knew I needed help. Since that moment of clarity, I've joined numerous genealogy support groups, where we offer each other strength and hope, along with research tips and potluck dinners. And I have finally admitted, to myself and to other human beings, that I am powerless over genealogy and my research has become unmanageable.

It may be too late for me. But, science has found that young family historians – those who are, as yet, only potential geneaholics – can sometimes stop in time.

Answer these questions to see if you are in the early stages of addiction.

1. **Home** *Has genealogical paperwork taken over any room in your house?*

2. **Friends** *Is genealogy interfering with your social life? Do people edge away from you at parties when you burst into tears over the 1890 U.S. census?*

3. **Family** *Do your relatives stare into space and hum nervously when you explain your latest research? Do you find dead people more fun than live ones?*

4. **Marriage** *Has your spouse ever asked "Aren't you done yet? How far back are you planning to go?"*

5. **Health** *Are you starting to show the physical and mental signs of genealogic deterioration, such as red-rimmed eyes, a loss of interest in current events, a shortened attention span for non-ancestral topics, excessive viewing of the History Channel?*

If you answered yes to even one of these questions, you are on the road to genealogical addiction. You must not research even one more ancestor! You must stop NOW . . . before it's too late!

When you feel an overwhelming urge to research, repeat the following until the urge goes away:

My mother found me in a cabbage patch. My mother found me in a cabbage patch. My mother found me in a cabbage patch.

Good luck and God help you.

A Little Jiffy, Practically Foolproof, Genealogical Organization System

(Pat. Pending)

t's that time of year when movie theaters fill up with action, adventure, horror and disaster films. (Actually, what time of year isn't?)

I think Hollywood is missing a good bet by ignoring the genealogy connection. One look at my den would provide enough plot material to fuel two dozen disaster flicks.

It all started innocently enough in 1995, when I wandered into a Family History Center for the first time. Three weeks later, I purchased a one-inch, three-ring notebook with six tabs, which I neatly labeled with six family surnames.

It's been spiraling out of control ever since.

A year later, after amassing photocopies, notebooks, reference books, syllabuses (syllabi?), computer printouts and other assorted genealogical flotsam, not to mention jetsam, I announced to my husband, "This thing is getting out of hand. We need to expand the house."

After a brief "discussion," which I won, I drew a little picture on graph paper and we hired a contractor, took out a mortgage and added some square footage to one end of the house, ballooning out from the den.

We put in floor-to-ceiling bookcases along one wall, hauled in a humongous metal storage cabinet in which to stash supplies, bought in two file cabinets, installed a big old rocking chair in which I planned to rock slowly back and forth, musing over my family group sheets, constructed a desk and a computer stand, placed ancestors' photos on the bookcase shelves for inspiration and on the seventh day, we rested, and saw that it was good.

On the eighth through the 1,825th day, we paid down the mortgage.

Now, 1,826 days later, I hop-scotch across the den floor, trying not to disturb the foot-high stacks of papers that cover most of the carpet.

The rocking chair was hauled out two years ago to make way for a dinette table and chairs, on which to stack yet more papers. The carpet that is not covered with papers is covered with portable file boxes in various stages of disarray. The ancestor photos have been removed to somewhere or other (I'll find them one of these days, I'm sure) to make room for yet more stacks of papers and notebooks.

In short, this thing has once again gotten out of hand. So, I explained to my husband the other day that what we need to do is for me to take over the garage.

This will be really inexpensive compared to building another addition onto the house, I pointed out, since the garage already exists.

All we have to do is put in drywall, install some nice windows and pretty French doors opening to the patio (because it really should look nice, right?), put in a nice tile floor or maybe some attractive carpeting, finish the ceiling and add recessed lighting and maybe a ceiling fan, build more wall-to-wall bookcases, get some bigger file cabinets, run high-speed data wiring and phone lines to the garage and maybe – I'm not sure about this yet – put in a fireplace.

The only problem is to find some place for my husband to store the personal items that he always keeps in the garage, like his lawn mower, Christmas ornaments, bags of fertilizer, rakes and shovels. I figure putting a little metal storage shed behind the garage should handle all that.

Anyway, this new organize-my-papers solution is once again in the preliminary, or "discussion," stage between my husband and me, and so far, the outcome is iffy. But, I'm sure that as soon as I can convince him that all the stuff now in the garage will fit into a storage shed, if we winnow it down just a wee bit, he will see the light.

We may have to compromise and get rid of the lawn mower, but that's why God invented ice plant. I mean, it's not like he enjoys cutting the grass. I would think this would be A Good Thing, and not the end of the world, as he seems to feel.

Anyway, I hope soon to begin finally (once and for all) to get a place for everything of a genealogical nature, with everything in its place.

And, if it should turn out that five years from now, I need yet another wall of book shelves and another bank of file cabinets, well, there's always the house next door.

Not to mention the storage shed.

Of course, if my husband fails to see the light about the garage, I'll just have to go immediately to Plan B: Sell my disaster plot to Hollywood, and hire some assistants to get my den organized – and keep it that way.

. . . where?

That Poor Man

My husband and I have a mixed marriage. I'm not talking about our political differences, nor our ethnic backgrounds, nor our religions, nor our different approaches to money.

No, the big, irreconcilable difference between us is that one of us is a genealogist and one of us is genealogically impaired. (Or, as he might put it, genealogically impaled.)

It seems to be a common urge among genealogists to seek out and marry someone without the family-history gene (known in medical circles as a "non-g"). It's a subtle, sadistic urge we genealogists get that science cannot explain.

I understand that in some jurisdictions of the U.S., springing an interest in genealogy on an unsuspecting spouse in midlife or later is automatic grounds for divorce under the category, "mental cruelty." I've also heard that in the trendier circles of New York and Hollywood, some spouses are writing a genealogy clause into their prenuptial agreements: "Any unilateral family-history research by either party shall result in mandatory marital counseling and/or the heavy sedation of both partners."

We don't need to turn to such extreme measures in our house, however, as my husband has learned to cope with his non-g condition bravely, which puts him way ahead of many other non-g's who are married to active genealogists.

A while back, I wrote a little essay for "Missing Links"[1] about organizing one's genealogy paperwork by building larger and larger additions to one's house to stash the mess. It seems that a number of female genealogists printed it out and brandished it at their long-suffering, non-g helpmates. I received several e-mails recounting the following scenario.

The wives had thrust the essay under their husbands' noses. "Here!" they cried. "Read this! I'm not so bad after all. I could be building additions to the house to store this mess, instead of just taking over the den!"

Their husbands read my essay, shook their heads and handed the essay back to their wives. "That poor man," they said, referring to my husband.

I didn't know whether or not to tell my husband about the responses. I don't want to encourage him in his geneaphobia, and I certainly don't want him to start thinking that his non-g condition is the "normal" human state. But, still, I thought it might buck him up to know

1.   A free online genealogy newsletter.

that there were others out there facing the same problems he has. He might feel better just knowing he was not alone.

I also heard from several male genealogists, who admitted that they were the addicted parties in their households, and that their wives were the ones lacking the genealogy gene – although this is a rarer combination. Usually, wives of genealogists catch the fever from their husbands pretty quickly. Although both genders can be afflicted, it is thought that women are more susceptible to the virus.

A marriage of a genealogically incompatible couple cannot be "fixed" except by painful, radical surgery (i.e., divorce), but it is possible for a non-g spouse to live a long and comfortable life, as long as the genealogist spouse is supportive and understanding. Usually, most of us genealogists treat our non-g spouses with the tender understanding we would hope for if we were the impaired partner. No one knows better than we do how divorce can clutter up a family group sheet. I help my husband cope by explaining to him daily how lucky he is.

For example, I tell him, he could be married to a shopaholic, who spends all day at the mall instead of at the Family History Center. This is a great argument to use when your spouse is feeling neglected because you're lavishing too much attention on dead people. Just remind him that, instead of worrying about your ancestors, none of whom will ever show up to spend the weekend, you could be out there spending money!

A close relative of mine was addicted to sailing, and I understood from his spouse that this is the recreational equivalent of tearing up your paycheck every week and throwing it in a lake. I use his example to point out to my husband that genealogy is not the only form of insanity that runs in my family – just one of the cheaper ones. "At least I'm not bugging you for a new spinnaker all the time," I tell him.

Other hobbies – compulsive gambling, or collecting rare coins, Van Goghs or Rembrandts – are even more expensive than shopping or sailing, and make building an occasional little addition onto the house for your genealogical files seem like a sensible and economical alternative.

Then there's bungee-jumping, sky-diving, race-car driving and spelunking. Imagine what would happen to our family's health insurance rates if I suddenly started leaping off bridges, jumping out of airplanes, turning left in a souped-up car at 180 mph or crawling into caves with a flashlight between my teeth. (Not to mention how hard it would be for me to get supper on the table if I were in midair, plummeting toward earth at dinnertime.)

In short, our non-g spouses could have it a lot worse than they do. As hobbies go, genealogy is a little weird, perhaps, and can be annoying to the non-g who has to listen to endless recitals of our research, but it's benign and not too terribly expensive.[2]

The major problem non-g spouses face is that – although it is believed to be an inborn trait – genealogy has also proved to be contagious.

Medical science has not yet explained how this works, but even the most resistant spouses can have their immunity weakened after years of exposure to a partner

---

2. *Except for the occasional research trip and/or additions to the house.*

suffering from one of the more virulent forms.

The first symptoms of infection usually appear about the time the genealogist starts researching the non-g's family. The first time you explain to your spouse when and where his great-grandparents arrived in this country, your non-g spouse may look up from the paper – may even put it down! – and say, "That's interesting. Tell me more."

To a genealogist, those are the sweetest words in the English language. What they really mean is, another genealogist has just been hooked.

LOIS JESEK

. . . the best of cemeteries, graves and tombstones

Take the Last Train to Pottsville

My co-workers and I were sitting around at lunch one spring talking about our vacations. One had just returned from spending April in Paris. Another was headed to Rome. Others had penciled in Hawaii, London, New York, Yosemite.

"Where are you going this year?" someone asked me.

"Rhosllannerchrugog," I said. (Or, at least, that's what I hope I said. My attempts to pronounce the Welsh double-el usually sound like what follows when the dentist says: "rinse and spit." I suspect the reason the Welsh carry umbrellas everywhere is not because it's likely to rain – although on any given day, it is – but because Wales is infested with American genealogists trying to pronounce Welsh place names.)

Silence ensued while my co-workers mopped up.

When everyone was dry again, one nervously asked, "And where might that be?"

"Near Mold."

A profound silence ensued. The people at the table

chewed uneasily. Finally, someone said, "Why are you going to . . . Mold?"

"To look at graves."

This resulted in a general stampede from the area. Which leads to my point: Attempting to describe the appeal of a genealogical field trip to non-genealogists can shut down a conversation faster than a tick suckin' blood from a Pedernales bedbug, or whatever it is that Texans say to indicate excessive speed.

I didn't used to be this way. In fact, I started out life as more or less a normal person looking for vacation ideas that entailed relaxation, such as lolling around on beaches of golden sand; or mental stimulation, such as visiting museums in exciting world-class cities; or spiritual uplift, such as viewing awe-inspiring cathedrals or the scenic wonders of national parks. You know, the usual meaningless, boring, touristy stuff.

Then I found genealogy, and it's been downhill ever since (and I don't mean on skiis).

My first genealogical field trip, a.k.a. "vacation," was to Pottsville, Pennsylvania, and I had a wonderful time. Found my great-great-grandfather's and great-great-grandmother's graves, and my great-grandpa's grave (Note to self: One of these days, go back and find out where the heck they put great-grandma), and lots of death records in the county courthouse, and a quit-claim deed to die for. Life doesn't get much better than that.

If my co-workers didn't quite understand my satisfaction with my trip, at least they had heard of Pottsville, because The Monkees once sang a song that sounded like it could have been written about Pottsville ("Last Train to Clarksville," which is very close). Where I lost them was showing off my vacation photographs, which consisted entirely of pictures of headstones – close ups, middle distance, long distance, at an angle, in sun, in shade, etc., with flowers and without. You know, the usual.

My next vacation was to Salt Lake City, which civilians can also accept, because there are all kinds of attractions in the area that normal people appreciate. After my

LOIS JESEK

fourth trip there, however, a friend said to me, "Boy, you must really like that lake," and I replied "There's a lake?"

47

My explorations of the city, of course, had been limited to the trudge across the alley from the hotel to The Library – a distance of some 20 feet – although once I did cross the street in the other direction to a mall to buy a new pen when mine ran out of ink.

Next vacation, I headed for Ashtabula County, Ohio, and it got harder to explain to real people why I was going there, because The Monkees never sang about Ashtabula, although they should have, because it's certainly as much fun as Pottsville/Clarksville and is certainly just as great a place to take a train from.

And, boy does Ashtabula have some great cemeteries! Hoo-boy. Talk about a blast from the past! (Whew! Excuse me, while I take a drink of water and try to get my pulse rate back to normal. Just thinking about it gets me all a-twitter).

From Ashtabula, it was a short step to Clearfield County, Pennsylvania, known far and wide for. . . uh . . . well, it's a very pretty neck of the woods, and I recommend it highly to anybody who has family planted in the area. And even to those who don't. Get off the turnpike and look around at this great country, for gosh sakes. See what's really out there. (And once you're in the area, I highly recommend spending an afternoon or two in the Odd Fellows Cemetery in Brisbin.)

But all of this was just a warm-up to going over the water to the mother lode. An entire nation chock full of dead ancestors plus dusty old libraries, tucked-away records offices, moss-covered cemeteries, tiny parish churches, etc., etc. Heaven on earth.

And, Mold, Wales, turned out to be just as charming as I knew it would be. And as for Rhosllannerchrugog –

well, what can you say about going "home" and walking the streets that generation after generation of your ancestors once walked?

If you're a genealogist, you get it. If you're not, there's no way you'll ever understand.

And, I'm a genealogist, folks. I'll take August in Ashtabula over April in Paris any day, any way.

Wanna see my pictures?

Now!
New, Improved
Genealogy
in a
Brand New Package!

I am hardly a genealogy expert, but even I can see that there's lots of room for improvement. If economics is called The Dismal Science, then genealogy has got to be considered The Downright Morbid Hobby. (All those dead ancestors, for starters. Give me a break.)

Although the end results of our genealogical efforts are gratifying, and produce cute little charts suitable for framing, the methodology is tedious, annoying, hard on the eyes and time-consuming.

The main problem with genealogy is that most of us are saddled with uncooperative, disorganized and generally poor-caliber ancestors. If we're going to improve genealogy, then, clearly, we need to improve our ancestors.

Ancestral Upgrades

I'm not suggesting that we trade in dear old g-g-g-g-whosiewhat for Marie Antoinette or Napoleon. That's silly. What I am suggesting is that we upgrade those inconsiderate ancestors who hid in the coal cellar when the census taker arrived, thinking the knock on the door was the tax man. The ones who thoughtlessly never bought land or left a forwarding address. Who "forgot" (ha, ha, very funny, grandpa) to post banns and christen the kids.

Surely, there are leftover ancestors somewhere who have been neglected despite having been compulsive record-keepers – who left reams of diaries, Bibles, deeds, wills, etc. These poor neglected chaps would be delighted, I'm sure, to be incorporated into some nice modern-day pedigree. Why struggle with lackadaisical ancestors who obviously didn't care a fig about us, when perfectly respectable, highly annotated ancestors are being wasted? Wasted, I tell you!

We see evidence of these well-behaved but under-utilized ancestors all over the place. They show up as the legible name on the census record, right above the smudge we suspect might be g-g-grandpa. The sibling whose every life achievement was recorded in minute detain – in still-vivid black ink – while his younger brother (the "birth ancestor" nature unfortunately assigned us)

Great-great grandmother and daughter Fifi
"Before Ancestral Clip Art"

barely made it into the margin of the family Bible in No. 3 pencil. Etc. Etc. Etc.

So, let's give ourselves permission to select the ancestors we truly deserve.

Ancestral Clip Art

All of us have some old photos that we can't identify. Why are these always the good-looking ones?

I have a picture of my great-grandmother that must have shattered the lens of that old wooden camera they used to photograph her. I'm surprised the state of

Great-great grandmother "After Ancestral Clip Art"

Ohio didn't ban photography for good when that thing was printed. You look at it and wonder just how desperate great-grandpa was to get . . . uh . . . married. Is it possible she was the only woman he'd ever seen? Did he have nothing for comparison?

And how did our family ever have the will to reproduce again after she came along? If ever there was a reason for a family to pack it in genetically, this was it.

The best explanation I can come up with is that she must have had one heck of a good personality. We're talking Mother Teresa and June Cleaver combined here.

And of course, house lighting was pretty poor in those days. And women wore veils a lot.

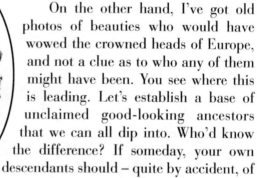

On the other hand, I've got old photos of beauties who would have wowed the crowned heads of Europe, and not a clue as to who any of them might have been. You see where this is leading. Let's establish a base of unclaimed good-looking ancestors that we can all dip into. Who'd know the difference? If someday, your own descendants should – quite by accident, of course – get your photo mixed up with Marilyn Monroe's or Brad Pitt's, would you really object?

Aren't you secretly hoping they will?

New Math

For those sticklers who don't care to upgrade their ancestors, let's establish some ground rules to handle ill-kept and/or offensive records.

If you can't read your ancestor's census entry, go three

lines above it and see if you can read that one. If not, continue back three lines at a time until you come to a legible entry. When you finally find something you can read, copy it out and footnote it thusly:

1870 Ohio census / Microfilm #whatever / Rule of Three

It sounds very official, doesn't it?

And should you encounter, as I have, ancestors so poor at basic arithmetic that they actually claimed a marriage date two years after the birth of their first child, you should correct the date of the marriage to nine months prior to the birth.

They'd do the same for you.

Of course, if what you like is the challenge of genealogy, then feel free to continue under the old rules. And, what the heck – why not raise the bar for your own descendants?

For instance, why not give all your kids the same first name, boys and girls alike.

Or take a lesson from my family, and give the kids first/ last name combinations that have been used already in seven consecutive generations. Make a deal with all your same-surname cousins to name their children alike. Insist on soft marble headstones in rainy climates. Use lots of cellophane tape to firmly affix old family photos to albums. Endorse census sampling.

We can, with very little effort, drive our descendants as nuts as our ancestors are driving us.

. . . family portraits

COUSINS BY THE DOZENS

When I was very young, my family attended a church where we were related to everyone but the organist's dog, and I never could figure out exactly how we all fit together relationship-wise, or even who everybody was. I just knew that everybody in the congregation outside of my nuclear family seemed to be an aunt, uncle, cousin or some other, even-more-exotic kinperson.

Then I grew up and discovered genealogy, and found that there are rules governing the degrees of kinship. All those baffling terms like, "first cousin once removed" and "double second cousins" follow simple, logical rules that anyone can master.

As a random act of genealogical kindness, I've created a quick guide to relationships. A cheat sheet, if you will. Memorize these simple rules, and you'll never again be at a loss for words when strangers you're related to hug you and say you look just like big ole' Billie Jean before she got so sick, poor thing, and how come you never write?

First cousin

Your first aunt or first uncle's first child. (A first aunt or uncle is defined as your parent's eldest sibling, known technically as the "oldest child." If your parent is the eldest, or an only child, and you are that parent's eldest, or only, child, then you are your own first cousin, and are probably spoiled rotten as a consequence. I've known plenty like you, and it's not a pretty sight.)

Second cousin

Your first aunt or uncle's second child, or your second aunt or uncle's first child. (A second aunt or uncle is the second-eldest child of any grandparent; note, however, that if your parent should him- or herself be the second child, then you and your brothers and sisters are second cousins primarily and siblings secondarily, and only at Thanksgiving. If you should happen to be the second child of two second children — boy, are you in trouble. Children who are their own double second cousins rarely turn out well.)

Third cousins

See definition of second cousins, and add one to every whole number. I'm sure you have caught the drift by now. Let's move on.

First-degree cousin

Cousin with a black belt. Usually treated with great respect by the rest of the family.

Double first cousins

Twin children of your first aunt or first uncle.

Double-dip cousin

Cousin who can't decide between chocolate and vanilla.

Double-knit cousin

Cousin dressed for "Casual Friday."

Doublemint cousins

Twin cousins who model for chewing gum ads.

First cousin once removed

Your first aunt or first uncle's first child who is now living with said aunt or uncle's divorced spouse.

First cousin twice removed.

Your first aunt or first uncle's first child who is now living with said aunt or uncle's divorced spouse in a different state.

First cousin once reproved

Obnoxious young relative who inspires such parental comments as, "Why can't you be more like your cousin Myron? He's only had one spanking in his entire life!"

First cousin twice reproved

Myron's naughty sibling.

First cousin once refurbished

First cousin with a nose job.

First cousin twice refurbished

A first cousin with a nose job and his or her "eyes done."

First cousin oft renovated.

What Michael Jackson is to his parents' siblings' children.

First cousin once resuscitated.

First cousin who almost drowned once, but didn't, thank heavens.

First cousin once recharged.

(A) A first cousin with a pacemaker, or
(B) A first cousin whose lawyer has never heard of double jeopardy.

First cousin once deranged, twice deranged, thrice deranged, etc.

We have so many of these in our family, I can hardly bear to define these terms, they bring back such painful memories. Let's just say, you know one when you see one and you don't know one when you are one.

Kissing cousin

The effusive type. Every family has at least one.

Dissing cousins

Cousins who talk nasty about the rest of the family behind their backs.

Here is an easy way to remember how to combine the "doubles," "triples," etc., with the "removeds" and other "re-" cousins. Just multiply all the numbers involved. Thus your double first cousin three-times deranged is, in kinship math, your deranged sixth cousin (2 [double] x1 [first] x 3 [deranged] = 6). You may get an argument on this from people who do not understand the subtleties of kinship math. Just explain that you read it in a book somewhere, so it's obviously true.

That's all there is to it!

Now, test yourself. What degree of kinship exists between the youngest of two children (Child X) of one parent (Parent A) who is a middle child of three, and another parent (Parent B), who is the eldest child of four of a second marriage, and the twin children (Children Y and Z) of Parent A's younger sister (Parent C) who has a pacemaker, a nose job and a fanny tuck, and who is married to an only child (Parent D) who talks nasty about the rest of the family behind their backs, but who has a black belt in judo, so no one complains? (Further necessary information: Child X cannot decide between chocolate, vanilla and strawberry.)

Give up?

Child X 's relationship to Children Y and Z is that of a dissing, first-degree, triple-dipping, double-third cousin once recharged and twice refurbished. Or, in kinship math, your 36th cousin (1 x 3 x 2 x 3 x 1 x 2 = 36).

Now, wasn't that easy?

As to the proper response when a stranger you're related to rushes up and hugs you and says you look just like big ole' Billie Jean before she got so sick, poor thing, and how come you never write?

Try, "Bug off." It works for me.

Great-Grandpa? Is that you? ? ?

Oh, Behave!

There are some ancestors who just won't take "No" for an answer. You try to be fair to all your forebears, following the twists and turns of the dullest of their lives with unflagging interest. But, eventually the time comes for you to move on to the next research subject. As the bumper sticker says: So many ancestors, so little time.

At this point, a decent forebear will let go graciously. But there are those ancestors who refuse to go gently into that dark hard drive. They cling to you like Saran wrap.

They barge to the head of the line, they cut in and they interrupt rudely. I suspect that these ancestors were probably just as annoying and demanding when they were alive as they are now that they are dead. Some people are improved by the passage of time, while others are beyond rehabilitation at any distance.

All of which brings me to great-grandfather X. (I don't want to use his real name in case his "shadow" is lurking nearby, reading over my shoulder, which it probably is. He's bad enough when he's trying to be helpful. I don't want to make him mad.)

It feels like this guy is stalking me. I need a restraining order, but I'm not sure how to explain it to a judge: "Yes, your honor, of course, I realize he's dead, *but he won't leave me alone.*"

If I could find a judge who's a genealogist, she'd understand instantly. But, in lieu of that, I'm urging our politicians to get busy (there's a concept!) and introduce some legislation guaranteeing that we genealogists are entitled to run our research as we see fit. Our ancestors get no say in the matter.

Great-grandpa is using the most ridiculous excuses to interrupt my necessary and legitimate research into other ancestors. While I am deeply appreciative of his efforts to help me so far, it's starting to scare me. Who knows where this might end?

This is the guy who, years ago, slyly guided my hand to the "wrong" shelf to pull down the "wrong" book that had an essential clue to his whereabouts. He's the one who arranged for the one person in the county who had the key to his story to mysteriously appear in the same courthouse office the same day and the same minute I arrived there from 3,000 miles away. He guided me to "his" cemetery on unmarked roads and directed me to a parking place about ten feet from his grave. He did everything but send up flares and fly a little flag from his headstone saying, "Yoo hoo, over here!"

For all this, I am very, very grateful. We can all use a little "Psychic Roots" help along the way – me more than most. I need every ounce of help I can get, from any source whatsoever.

But, in great-grandpa's case, I feel I already know as much about him as I really want to find out – in fact, I've got more than I care to put in Ye Olde Family History. I not only know all the begats and the vitals, the hithers and yons, I also know bits and pieces about his home life that would never land him a starring role in "Father Knows Best," if you get my drift.

But, although I consider myself done with him, he is apparently not yet done with me.

Until a few weeks ago, there was one piece of the puzzle that I had not been able to find; one tiny factoid in his story that remained missing – which is: How did he get from Point A (North Wales) to Point B (Western Pennsylvania).

I knew approximately when he came, because his naturalization petition gave me the day, month and year that he arrived in the port of New York. I say, "I knew *approximately*" because, while his petition claimed he arrived in the port of New York on Dec. 23, 1871, he is nowhere to be found in the passenger lists for that date and port.

Nevertheless, for the past few years, I've been celebrating Dec. 23 as "Great-grandpa Lands in America Day," making a toast at dinner in memory of the brave little Welsh family, huddled together in a bleak hotel room, on a cold and blustery New York winter day, thousands of miles from hearth and home, exhausted, alone frightened, not knowing what was in store for them.

Silly me.

I'd checked the passenger lists a zillion times. I'd gone through every ship's arrival log for 365 days both backwards and forwards from the target date. I'd checked Philadelphia, Boston, Baltimore and any other Atlantic port I could find for those years, in case great-grandpa thought all American cities were named "New York." No great-grandpa.

So, sensibly, I decided that he'd snuck into the country under an assumed name and I prepared to move on.

But, this is not an ancestor you can just toss aside. He is *ready* to be researched, he picked *me* to research him and he is not going to let me go until he says I'm done.

Thus, it came to pass that on a recent summer Sunday, I headed to a nearby Family History Center, innocently preparing to start looking for new and interesting ancestors. I traveled light, carrying only some notes with which to begin my research into my husband's family. They had arrived in Seattle early in the last century. I knew that the center would naturally have microfilm copies of all the Seattle passenger lists from the beginning of time. That was where I planned to start.

You'll note in the above paragraph that this was a Sunday. The center was closed to the public, except for the members of a local genealogy society, who were assembling for a monthly meeting. I walked brazenly in under the pretense of attending the meeting, then immediately slunk into the microfilm area.

Alone in the gloom of the dimly lit microfilm room, I

discovered to my surprise that there were no Seattle passenger lists there at all. By the time I was convinced of this, the meeting was well underway, and it was being held smack dab outside the microfilm area. I could not leave the room without shoving aside the speaker, and clomping through the middle of the meeting, revealing myself to one and all as the kind of snarky genealogist who hides out in the microfilm catacombs during society meetings, furtively researching while her betters are taking care of business. There was no other exit. I was trapped. *Trapped.* The meeting could go on for hours. What to do, what to do? How to while away the time without blowing my cover?

OK, I thought wearily, as long as I'm here, I'll give great-grandpa one more shot.

Crouching behind the darkened readers so that no one in the meeting could see my guilty shadow on the wall, I crept to the New York Ships Passenger Lists microfilm cabinet (which I know by heart), to once again go through the same stupid lists I've read a million times.

You know what's coming, of course.

On his naturalization petition, great-grandpa had written the date of his arrival as Dec. 23, 1871. I had already searched every ship list between Dec. 23, 1870, and Dec.23, 1872 looking for his family group. Several times. I had always figured that at least the day and the month would have been right, right?

Silly me.

I sighed and loaded the 1872 film into the reader. Starting at Dec. 23, 1872, listlessly cranking the reader, I was listening to the speaker a few feet away, hardly looking at the film. It took me about five minutes to reach Dec. 30 – where (almost) the whole dang family was listed. The wife, the kids, the baby.

Only great-grandpa was missing. But that was his family all right. Unmistakable. Names, ages and origins matched perfectly. So great-grandpa hadn't come over with his family.

That means – uh, lemme work this out – he must have come over alone.

So, why did he write the wrong day and year on his naturalization petition? Could it possibly be just another example of (gasp) human error? What?!? Error in genealogical records? Hard to believe.

It was only later that the implications of all of this sank in.

Great-grandpa is taking more and more extreme measures to keep me researching him. Luring me to a Family History Center on a Sunday under false pretenses!

Misleading me about the Seattle passenger lists! Trapping me in the microfilm room like a cornered rat! Forcing me to once again look through records I had already worn out with searching! Are there any lengths to which this man will not go, to make me fill in his life story?

The problem is, it worked. He's got my attention again.

Hopefully, when I get those last pesky details discovered, such as when he himself came over and where the family was staying after he left Wales, etc., that will finally be the end of it and I can get back to research on other branches of the family.

Right, great-grandpa?

Great-grandpa???

. . . promises, promises, promises

Be It Hereby
RESOLVED . . .

I wrote my letter to Santa (a.k.a., my genealogical wish-list) really early this year, with a cc: to my husband to be on the safe side, and on Christmas morning, I leapt out of bed, dashed past the tree and packages and out to the garage, where I flung open the door. And what to my wondering eyes should appear, but the same old flotsam that had been there the day before. Musty, dusty garden equipment, sacks of fertilizer and grass seed, tools, lumber, broken-down treadmills, and unopened mystery boxes from when we moved into the house 27 years ago.

Inexplicably – go figure – the garage had not been magically transformed into the dazzling genealogical library/workshop/office that I had asked of Santa. Piffle.

However, I persevere in my efforts to get organized. Since Santa Baby has fizzled on me yet again, I am proceeding to Plan B in getting my genealogical mess in order. I am making a modest little list of resolutions for the new year. Thus will I motivate myself to get a grip on this genealogy thing.

1. **I RESOLVE**: To institute a brand new filing system that will once and for all put every piece of genealogy-related paper in its place, neatly labeled and filed. Of course, I have to figure out some kind of filing system first, but when I do, watch out, world!

2. **I RESOLVE**: To thereupon use my new system (whatever it may turn out to be) to label and file away every factoid I obtain in the future.

3. **I RESOLVE**: To finally write it all down. Get the Great American Family History Novel underway at last.

4. **I RESOLVE**: To decide on one genealogy program and actually learn to use it, and get all my data entered, all my photos scanned, all my footnotes in place, etc. Then I will produce reams of nifty charts suitable for framing, which I will distribute to cousins around the globe, whether they want them or not. In fact, whether they even admit we're related or not. (I'm getting stiff resistance in some quarters. You know how that goes.)

5. Regarding Resolution 4, **I RESOLVE**: to learn to use the scanner I bought three years ago. (Is it too late to register it? If not, I'll even register it.)

6. **I RESOLVE**: To get my research notes, scraps, and scribblings organized, and to set up (and to

use faithfully thereafter) a research log.

7. **I RESOLVE**: To set up a calendar of expiration dates for my memberships in various genealogical and historical societies, and thus eliminate those embarrassing gaps in my memberships and/or pesky reminder notices.

8. **I RESOLVE**: To read in their entirety all the genealogical journals I have received in the past six years, not just the jokes; to clip the pertinent articles (and, naturally, organize and file them neatly away as I do so), then ruthlessly discard the rest of each journal, no matter how convinced I am that I will need every page of it some day.

9. **I RESOLVE**: To check my e-mail boxes daily, and read all my newslist messages promptly, saving all important information in a timely manner and deleting the rest.

10. **I RESOLVE**: To focus my research on one ancestor at a time. I will relentlessly pursue that one person until all avenues of research are exhausted, at which point, I will mark the file "finis" and move on to someone else – and never look back.

11. And, since man does not live by genealogy alone (it just seems that way), in regard to other pressing matters, **I hereby RESOLVE**: to lose 20 pounds, join a gym and exercise three times a week, eat five servings of vegetables and/or fruit every day, eliminate red meat from my diet, learn to love tofu, dust and vacuum the house by Easter, keep my cholesterol under 200, read "A Remembrance of

Things Past" in its entirety (it is about genealogy, isn't it?), try adventurous new recipes with exotic ingredients, learn Welsh, repaint the living room, and work to bring about world peace and universal tolerance.

I plan to get started on all this the first thing in the morning January 1, right after the Rose Parade. Well, of course, I have to take the tree down first and make lunch, but how long can that take? And just to show how serious I am about all this, I'm going to leap up from the computer this very minute and take a nap, thus starting immediately to conserve my energy and build up my strength and stamina for the Big Moment.

LOIS JESEK

The Enron Ancestor

When the census man came up the drive,
To see if great-gramps was alive,
Did my ancestor crouch
Out of sight by the couch?
Or did records just never survive?

When the tax agent knocked on the door,
To see if great-grandpa owed more,
Did my ancestor run
And grab him a gun,
And leave the man dead on the floor?

Enron thinks it invented the shredder,
But great-grandpa, he got there ahead-er.
Gramps' records are gone,
Missing, kaput, so long!
And the paper trail couldn't be deader.

The Society of GENEALOGICAL Research

. . . unaccustomed as I am to . . .

LOIS JESEK

The
Six Stages of Death
by
Public Speaking

(With deepest apologies
to Dr. Elisabeth Kubler-Ross)

I will agree to anything, as long as it's far enough ahead. You want me to jump out of an airplane without a parachute while playing a bagpipe, and land in a river full of piranhas? When? Oh, not until October? Sure, put me down.

And I pencil in a note on my "to do" list to sign up for bagpipe lessons in September and buy a can of piranha repellent, and off I go, whistling into the sunset, confident that this year, October will never come.

That's why I agreed to give a little talk at my local genealogical society. They asked me so far in advance that I figured it would never actually happen. These talks are something we all have to do at some point, a sacrifice we all must perform at the altar of Holy Mackerel, the Goddess of Serendipity, to ensure bountiful harvests at the Family History Library when next we visit Salt Lake City.

As at most societies, at ours everybody pitches in to help the program person. I agreed to do my part, first because everybody in the society is so nice and helpful; second, because I thought it would sound churlish to say, "Are you out of your mind, woman? I have terminal stage fright"; third, because I truly feel we should do our part for genealogy when asked; and fourth and mostly, because she asked me in January to speak in April. That's a long, long time away.

Thus did I enter the first of the six stages of death by public speaking.

Stage One: Denial

This lasted from the moment I said yes to about two weeks before the appointed date, when I entered Stage One-B: Isolation. This was triggered by an e-mail from the program woman saying, "Everything all set?"

Chills ran down my spine. All that was missing was the background music from the shower scene in "Psycho." Shrieking violins would have captured my reaction perfectly. Good heavens, I remembered, The Speech! Can it be April already? Did they really mean *this year?* Whatever happened to January, February and March?

Now, what?

I hit delete while my brain raced for a solution.

"Don't open any e-mail for a while," I told my husband. "Don't answer the phone. It might be Them."

"Them who?"

"The genealogists."

"I thought you liked genealogists."

"Please! I don't want to talk about it."

Denial and isolation turned quickly to . . .

Stage Two: Anger

"Why, why, why, why? When will I ever learn? Bang, bang, bang." (This latter being the sound of my head hitting the wall). "What am I going to talk about? Piffle! Phooey! Fiddle-dee-dee!" (I'm translating my actual comments into language fit for family reading.)

Stage Three: Bargaining

Bargaining followed immediately thereafter, once my head-banging headache cleared up. Bargaining involved once again pinning my hopes on my husband. You'd think I'd have learned by now, but noooo, I continue to believe that the ultimate purpose of marriage is to give you an out.

"If I promise to learn to cook, will you call them and tell them I'm in the hospital?" I wheedled. "If I lose ten pounds, will you write them a note saying I left town suddenly and you don't know when I'll be back? Mention that I cleared out the bank account." (Which I do periodically, anyway, so it wouldn't really be a lie.)

Alas, I have the misfortune to be married to a man of sterling character who refuses to bail me out of my genealogy-induced misfortunes, so this approach proved futile. This led to . . .

Stage Four: Frantic Activity

(While this is not a part of Dr. Elisabeth Kubler-Ross' five stages of grief, it's certainly an important element in coping with dying in front of an audience.)

Stage Four was characterized by hours at the keyboard, typing, deleting, starting over, typing, deleting and starting over, all accompanied by moans, groans,

LOIS JESEK

sighs and whimpers. Eventually, desperation prevailed and a sort-of speech emerged, only to be followed by the realization that there also needs to be a handout. Egads and gadzooks! Long hours at the keyboard were replaced by long hours at the bookshelf, desperately searching for something to back up the half-cocked theories I planned to unload on my unsuspecting audience. One week before the talk . . .

Stage Five: Depression

took over. I noticed suddenly that life is but a wretched dream, made of sound and fury, signifying nothing. This was news to me, and I was amazed by this development. Wars. Pestilence. Famine. Terrorism. Sickness. Death. Futility was all around. How could I possibly talk about genealogy as if it mattered at a time like this? We were all doomed. *Doomed!*

My depression deepened as The Day rushed at me. I realized that in the unlikely event that I survived the address, and was not stoned to death by shocked and out-raged audience members, I would never again be able to show my face at the Society. I would be cut off from the genealogical community forever, having been discovered to be the ridiculous, contemptible, ignorant, foolish genealogical fraud I truly am.

Gloom overtook me. I almost (but not quite) lost my appetite. Trying to keep up my strength for the ordeal ahead, I forced myself to eat chocolate. Finding that a lit-tle chocolate didn't work, I ate a lot, trying to get my endorphins to kick in.

Finally, the day dawned.

To convey that scene, I will quote from John Greenleaf Whittier's poem "Snowbound," which I was forced to memorize in ninth grade. (As you read it, notice the alliteration of the "D's" in the first line and also how "drear" sort of rhymes with "cheerless." This was considered great stuff 50 years ago.)

The dawn that drear December day.
Rose cheerless over skies of gray.

Substitute "Smogbound" for "Snowbound" and April for December, and you've got the picture. The escape hatch had clanged shut.

The Sixth Stage: Acceptance

. . . arrived with the morning paper.

My husband and I ate breakfast in silence.

"You'll do fine," he said at last, looking up from the sports page. I smiled wanly, pityingly. He knows so little of the vast expertise of the people to whom I would be displaying my vast ignorance.

On the drive there, I reminded myself that it couldn't possibly be any worse than the root canal I had had done once, where the root was twisted and bent and the dentist had obviously gone to dental school because he couldn't get into jackhammer school. Remembering that root canal has gotten me through many a pickle.

The next few hours are a merciful blur.

Late that afternoon, back home and safely back in the First Stage – Denial – I skipped about our backyard, reborn. Birds sang. Squirrels did squirrely things. Roses arose. Butterflies fluttered by. My husband rolled his eyes.

Genealogy and I had both survived. Nobody had demanded my membership card and ripped it up in front of my face. Not one single rotten tomato had been tossed my way. Not one boo had been heard. Everyone had been kind and polite.

And – best of all – it was over!

"See, I told you it would be fine," my husband said.

"Nothing to it," I agreed.

Bring on the piranhas.

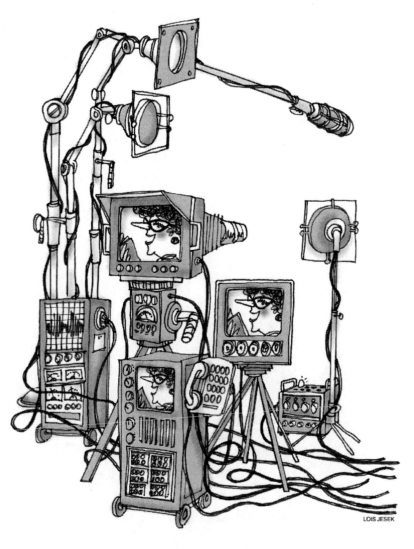

. . . "take 1,000, scene 4."

"I Dream of GENEALOGY"

or, How I Learned to Stop Worrying and Love TV

N o one was more surprised than I was to find myself involved with "Ancestors 2," the second year of the hit PBS genealogy series.

After only a couple of years of intermittent research, I'm still what real genealogists call a "newbie." The fact that I have stumbled across a few ancestral factoids here and there is mainly due to my continuing streak of beginner's luck. As my Midwestern father often said: "Even a blind pig finds an acorn sometime."

But as it turned out, this year, the producers were more interested in ancestors' stories than in genealogists' expertise, and that's how I slipped in.

Now that the filming session is over (whew!) and I am back to what passes for normal life in L.A., I can report that both genealogy and I seem to have survived. The odds are that "Ancestors 2" will also recover from the encounter, and members of the film crew will someday be able to smile wanly, sit up and begin taking nourishment again.

Just kidding.

It started when a writer from the Ancestors show read through the "Missing Links" archives looking for stories for this year's series. (And, THIS is why you should get those e-mails off to "Missing Links," "Rootsweb Review" and other e-zines, children, relating your successes!)

I was one of those she contacted, and when I stopped hyperventilating, I thought about it long and hard. In fact, I hesitated for almost five seconds before e-mailing back that I guessed I could be persuaded to participate. It's hard to type while fluttering your eyelashes and digging your toe shyly in the dirt, but I managed it.

Phone calls and interviews followed, each one ending with a warning from the show's producers that a lot of stories were being considered, that they were striving for balance and variety and that I could be rejected at any time. As the months passed, however, I began to suspect that I was the only Welsh-English-French-Manx-coal-miner's great-granddaughter they had been able to dig up. It may be an obscure ethnic niche to occupy, but it's exclusive.

Finally, it was settled. The story of g-grandfather Benjamin Ellis' untimely death (he was killed in a coal mine a couple of years after he brought his little family to the U.S.) and the struggles of his young widow and children to survive alone in a strange land would be included. The family had moved from Pennsylvania to Ohio after he died, and the date and location of Ben's death were unknown to later generations. My search for his grave would be the genealogical theme.

And so it came to pass, in the fullness of time, that The Big Day arrived.

The short version of what followed can be summed up like this: After you spend three months lying awake at night worrying about what they are going to ask you, you spend two hours in front of a camera, feeling like a deer caught in the headlights. Sweating up a storm, your mind wanders, your voice trails off in mid-sentence and you forget what they just asked or what you started to answer.

After that, you get to spend three months lying awake at night again, thinking of all the brilliant things you should have said – instead of whatever dumb thing you did say – if you'd only thought of them.

The best thing that came out of this is that I now know the answer to Freud's infamous question, "What do women really want?" The answer is: "A good listener!"

The reason I know this is because I finally met one. During the interview, the director and interviewer, Matt Whittaker, fixed me with a rapt, sympathetic, empathetic, hanging-breathlessly-on-every-word gaze. I could tell he was really pulling for me to sputter out the answers and/or complete a sentence, whichever came first. It was the male version of the spell-bound look Nancy Reagan used to bestow on Ronnie as she listened to his stock political speech for the 10,000th time.

If my husband would just once listen to my dinner conversation with that same look of fascination, approval and wordless encouragement on his face, I'd think I'd died and gone to heaven.

That was the high point. But, I quickly discovered, the filming wasn't going to consist only of an interview, as I had expected. I was, it turned out, required to "act."

They filmed me doing this and they filmed me doing that, and we traveled all over the map. After a while, I kind of lost track. I think my finest moment was The Trudge up the Courthouse Steps. I tried it with a little skip in my step; I tried it brisk and businesslike; I tried it languidly, my hand trailing behind me on the railing; I tried it with a saucy toss of my curls. It occurred to me later that they probably wanted the Plain Old Genealogy Slump – the way we all look at the end of the day, carrying 200 pounds of notebooks and file folders in a shoulder-bag – but I didn't have time to work out a Method-acting approach to any of the scenes. It was improv all the way.

Twelve hours after we started, we ended the filming in a cemetery. I said nervously, "I hope you don't want me to fling myself across a grave, sobbing 'Great-grandpa, great-grandpa! I've found you at last!' " (Oops, I just gave away the ending.) But fortunately, they just wanted me to walk around aimlessly, and I managed to do so without tripping over any low-lying headstones, or otherwise humiliating myself. Or at least, without humiliating myself any more than I had already done during the iced-tea incident at lunch (don't ask; I'm not going to tell you everything).

One of the final shots was me staring into space, lost in thought. They said later that I did that really well, but it wasn't hard. The glassy-eyed, faraway stare is something I mastered in ninth grade algebra class. It's one of those things you never forget how to do – like falling off a bicycle.

What I was mulling over during the shot was the burning question: Who should play the role of the Genealogist Wanna-Be (me) when the story comes to the big screen? I had narrowed the choices to Cindy Crawford and Julia Roberts, and had just about decided on Roberts – who, I feel, has the acting chops for the big graveyard scene – when the three most beautiful words in the English language rang out. "It's a wrap!"

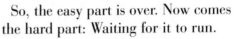

So, the easy part is over. Now comes the hard part: Waiting for it to run.

Assuming that great-grandpa and I make it past the dreaded cutting-room floor, that is, and are selected for the final series. The uncertainty never ends.

Should it happen, however, I already have my defense ready. "Who on earth was that weird old woman," I will ask, with a brave attempt at a Julia Roberts smile, "who was impersonating me on Ancestors 2?" [1]

---

1.   It did run, by the way, but Julia Roberts still won't return my calls.

LOIS JESEK

Living the Lifestyle

Once upon a time, a long, long time ago, (OK, it was 1995), I was a fresh-faced, eager, young[1] genealogy newbie. Gung-ho as all get out. Ready to find and prove beyond a reasonable doubt every last name, date, place, sibling, neighbor and event ever connected to Ye Olde Family Tree. Ready to nail it all down and ship it on out.

I planned to assemble my flawless research (once I finished it, of course) into a camera-ready family saga, notable both for its impeccable citations and its sparkling prose. Could a collection of family group sheets and fan charts ever win a Pulitzer Prize? I aimed to find out.

But, alas, as John Lennon once said, "Life is what

1. Compared to a Sequoia.

happens while we're busy making other plans." [2] In my case, research is what happens only when I'm not busy at the local genealogy society doing something else.

Somehow, betwixt my grand intentions, my great expectations and my camera-ready prose, it's all gotten away from me. My research has slowed to a crawl. And it's an occasional crawl, at that.

I blame my genealogy society for this sad state of affairs.

What happened was, I volunteered.

When I met up with the Society, it was love at first sight. That is, I fell in love with them. They were noticeably less impressed with me – but the rule of thumb of every genealogy society is, *If a volunteer's a'breathin', he ain't a'leavin'.*

At one point, they asked members for volunteers to help with the journal, and I allowed as how I was available for the occasional stint. You can tell I was never in the Army, where you quickly learn to hold your breath and stand rigidly at attention, staring straight ahead, when the call goes out for volunteers to balance apples on their heads while the sergeant field tests a new bazooka.

"Aha!" I thought. "Volunteer work! What a great idea! Here's a way to learn more about research from the undoubted experts in the field, as well as pay back a little of what I've so generously been given by those genealogists who went before me."

A noble sentiment, you'll agree.

---

2. Doesn't sound like him, does it? But I keep seeing this on the Internet, so it must be true.

That was in 2000. I have barely opened my research notebooks since.

The only way I can get any research done is to leave town. Leaving the country is even better. But short of a trip abroad, a trip to some domestic genealogical site will do in a pinch (Salt Lake City springs to mind), if I don't leave a forwarding address, and don't take my cell phone with me.

What's scary is that I'm the least involved of all the volunteers I meet at the Society. No matter what day I show up at the office, I see many of the same people working the phones, helping the (usually non-dues-paying) customers, indexing, collating, stamping books, teaching classes, filing, mailing, keeping ledgers, scheduling or holding meetings, unjamming the copy machines, putting fresh toilet paper in the restrooms and doing the million other mundane things that the Society needs done to function at its penny-pinching, basic-sustenance level.

What's even scarier is that, until a few months ago, I was working at a "real" job full time, squeezing everything of a genealogical nature in on weekends and evenings.

That was my excuse then for not advancing my research. I figured that, once I retired, I would finally have lots of time for research, plus doing my work at the Society, plus "getting a life," whatever that might entail.

A year ago, I explained my plan to several people.

"I'm going to retire soon," I told them, "So I'll have lots of time to work on my family history, volunteer, go to movies and plays, get my garden into shape, organize the den and take up ceramics. Plus which, I'll finally have time to write the Great American Historical Novel, as soon as I finish my research!"

To which the answer almost universally was: "Hah!"

I say "almost." One friend nodded sagely, and agreed.

"Yeah, that'll be great," she said "I'll be doing the same thing myself soon."

It goes without saying that she had not retired yet, either. She's now getting closer to that red-letter day, however, and fully intends to devote herself to her genealogical research full time, while spending "a little time" as a genealogical society volunteer.

HAH!

I don't have the heart to tell her that it doesn't work that way. I have seen first hand how volunteering expands like an inflatable life raft whooshing out of its envelope and knocking aside everything in its path. I suspect that my friend, like me, is doomed to live the Genealogical Lifestyle to the hilt.

What is the Genealogical Lifestyle?

Genealogists come in three flavors: hobbyists, professionals and those Living the Lifestyle

Here's how you tell us apart.

1. **Genealogy as a hobby** is where most of us start, and where the lucky (?) few remain. Genealogical hobbyists research their own family trees and communicate their findings to interested relatives. They do what they

can when they can, and they don't worry about it the rest of the time. Most of the time, the hobbyist passes for a normal human being. It's only when the subject of family history comes up that their nostrils flare and their faces flush, indicating that they have the virus in their system, and if they're not careful, it may lead to a full-blown attack of Genealogy Lifestyle.

2. **Genealogy as a profession.** All it takes is an IQ of 500+, an obsessive-compulsive personality and decades of studying and researching to achieve this exalted state. When you've thoroughly prepared yourself with all these years of work and study, you take a few tests that put the bar and medical board exams to shame, and, *voila*, you're now qualified to do research that is far beyond the capabilities of mere hobbyists. This makes you very, very rich.[3]

3. **Genealogy as a Lifestyle.** This state is easy to achieve. You just let the hobby take over your life. You spend every waking moment thinking about genealogy, talking about genealogy, writing about genealogy, reading about genealogy, taking genealogy classes, volunteering for genealogical organizations, attending genealogy events – and wondering when the heck you'll ever again find the time to do some actual research.

3.   Doesn't it?

If you'd like to sample the Genealogy Lifestyle, then come on down to your local society. They can surely use some help on their journal and in their office – and the restroom is probably out of soap again.

All the Cookies You Can Eat

*Or, How to Publish
a Genealogy Newsletter*

Most genealogy societies publish newsletters, journals or quarterlies of some sort. If you're responsible for getting one of these publications into print and into the mail, here's a simple checklist that will help you do so with maximum efficiency and effectiveness. Check each step off as you complete it.

Step 1 – Eight weeks before deadline

- Post a businesslike notice on the bulletin board asking for volunteers to help edit and print the newsletter, and add that you are looking for compelling, well-written, impeccably researched articles.

- Send an e-mail to all members explaining the same thing.

- At your society's monthly meeting, stand up and explain the same thing.

Step 2 – Six weeks before deadline

- Post a bigger notice on the bulletin board, asking for volunteers to help edit and print the newsletter, and explain that you need interesting articles.

  - Make the notice friendly and informal, to put potential volunteers at ease. Sample: "Hey, gang, here's your chance to help edit and print the society newsletter!!"

Be sure to use lots of exclamation points !!!

Explain that you will bake "delicious cookies" for all who help out. Underline "delicious."

- Send an e-mail to all members in the above format.

Step 3 – Four weeks before deadline

- Rip all other announcements from the bulletin board and replace them with a Help Wanted banner urging members to volunteer, and begging for articles.

- Use 72-point type and crimson ink for the banner. Leave a plate of cookies nearby, promising "lots more where these came from."

- Send another e-mail to all members pleading

for articles, and urging volunteers to step forward. Use all caps. Write "ALL THE COOKIES YOU CAN EAT" in the subject line of your message.

- At the monthly society meeting, bring cookies. Once the members are seated, lock the doors, including the restrooms.

- Announce at the start of the meeting that you need articles, plus volunteers to help put out the publication. Explain that the doors will not be unlocked until you have some names on the sign-up list.

  - Pass around the sign-up list.

  - At the end of the meeting, pass around the sign-up list again. Threaten to swallow the keys to the restrooms if no one signs up.

    - Lead the applause when two new members, attending their first-ever genealogy society meeting, say they guess they could write something.

(For the sake of this checklist, we'll call them Volunteer A and Volunteer B.)

- Unlock the doors, and jump back as the stampede for the restrooms thunders past.

Step 4 – Three weeks before deadline

- Send e-mail to volunteers
  A and B to remind
  them that their articles are
  due the following week.

- E-mail all other members
  pleading for help editing,
  printing and mailing the
  newsletter. Write in all caps.
  Explain again about the cookies.

Step 5 – Two weeks before deadline

- E-mail volunteers A and B,
  reminding them in a friendly,
  cheerful manner that their
  articles are due TODAY !!!!

- E-mail all other members,
  groveling for help editing, printing
  and mailing the newsletter.
  Format message as in previous
  two steps. Explain that – in addition
  to cookies – complimentary wine and
  cheese will be served throughout
  the editing process.

Step 6 – Twelve days before deadline

- Leave hysterical telephone
  messages for volunteers A
  and B to explain that your
  e-mail messages to them were
  returned marked, "User
  Unknown-Invalid Address."

Step 7 – Ten days before deadline

- Call phone company to see why volunteers A and B's phones have been disconnected.

Step 8 – Nine days before deadline

- Bake cookies.
  Eat them.

Step 9 – Eight days before deadline

- Telephone all current and past society members sobbing that you must have some kind of article from somebody – anybody. Leave messages explaining the situation at length. Explain that the articles do not have to be in English.

Step 10 – Seven days before deadline

- Bake cookies.
  Eat them.

Step 11 – Six days before deadline

- Visit local Family History Center at dawn. Accost every patron who arrives throughout the day, begging for articles. Explain that articles do not have to be in English and need not necessarily relate to genealogy.

Step 12 – Five days before deadline

- Repeat Step 11.

Step 13 – Four days before deadline

- Visit local Family History Center at dawn. Pore through entire collection of periodicals. Photocopy all likely articles to reprint.

Step 14 – Three days before deadline

- Visit homeless shelters, promising cheese, wine and cookies to anyone willing to help edit a genealogy newsletter. Explain what genealogy is. Add that volunteers do not need to speak, writeor understand English to qualify as editors.

Step 15 - Two days before deadline

- Attempt to track down publishers of photo-copied materials, asking permission to reprint articles. Leave polite messages at those publications still in existence.

- Bake cookies. Eat them.

Step 16 - One day before deadline

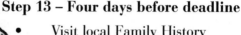

- Leave second set of messages for publishers of photocopied materials.

- Buy wine and cheese.

- Sample wine and cheese to verify quality.

Step 17 - Deadline Day!

- Log onto Internet,track down genealogy e-zines that allow reprints.

- Cut and paste, cut and paste, cut and paste.

- Download, download, download.

- Make a batch of cookie dough. Eat it.

- Make a second batch of cookie dough.

- Bake cookies. Eat them.

Step 18 - One day past deadline

- Cut and paste, cut and paste, cut and paste.

- Download, download, download.

- Bake cookies. Eat them.

- Bake more cookies. Eat them.

- Eat cheese.

Step 19 - Two days past deadline

- Eat cookie crumbs and cheese rinds.

- Uncork wine.

Lay out newsletter.

Step 20 – Three days past deadline

- Uncork remaining wine.

- Proofread newsletter.

Step 21 - Four days past deadline

- Find a designated driver to transport you and the camera-ready pages to the printer.

Step 22 – Six days past deadline

- Call printer to find out when newsletter will be ready. Maintain a friendly, cheerful tone of voice.

Step 23 – Eight days past publication deadline

- Call printer. Beg for newsletter to be done "soon."

Step 24 – Nine days past deadline

- Call printer. Leave stern message, insisting that newsletter be done "next." Explain your situation in great detail.

Step 25 – Ten days past deadline

- Call printer. In a wheedling tone of voice, offer to deliver cookies, cheese and wine to the print shop if newsletter is printed "next."

Step 26 – Eleven days past deadline

- Buy more wine and cheese.
  Bake cookies.

- Call print shop.
  Discuss situation with printer
  until he hangs up.

Step 27 – Twelve days past deadline

- Storm print shop.
  Barricade self in restroom
  with cookies, cheese and
  wine and threaten to not come
  out until newsletter is done.

Step 28 – Thirteen days pastdeadline

- Stagger from restroom, call designated
  driver to pick up you and the
  now-completed newsletter.

Step 29 – Fourteen days past deadline

- Affix mailing labels to newsletters.

Step 30 – Fifteen days past deadline

- Mail newsletters

Step 31 – Seventeen days past deadline

- Field complimentary phone calls and e-mails
  from grateful members who (with great
  reluctance, and trying only to be helpful)
  also take the opportunity to point out the
  multiple errors on each page.

- Mix large batch of cookie dough.
  Eat raw.

Step 32 – One month past deadline
and eight weeks before next deadline

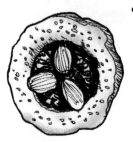

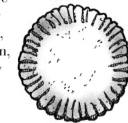

- Post a business-like notice on the bulletin board asking for volunteers to help edit and print the newsletter, and add that you are looking for compelling, well-written, impeccably researched articles.

- Send an e-mail to all members explaining the same thing.

- At your society's monthly meeting, stand up and explain the same thing.

Continue with steps 2-32.

And that's all there is to it!

All the Cookies You Can Eat

LOIS JESEK

LOIS JESEK

Ten Commandments of Genealogy

Or, Do as I Say-eth, Not as I Did-eth

I t has been suggested that a few words of advice to new genealogists about how to get started would be appropriate. There are many more-qualified people around to get advice from than me – plus which, I figure that any budding genealogists have surely dropped this book and run screaming from the room long before now. But in the event that any of you are still with me, here are my own Ten Commandments of Genealogy.

1.

Thou shalt start with thyself and worketh thy way backwards.

There are all kinds of ways to start your research. You can poke around on the Internet, or check the IGI (International Genealogical Index), etc. But sooner or later, you will need to start researching in original documents in a systematic way. Censuses are the most productive jumping-off place, and they provide lots of practice in loading a microfilm reader and groping around in the dark.

If you choose to start with censuses, start with your parents, siblings and grandparents and look in the most recent U.S. census that pertains to them (the 1930 is the most recent available), and only then move backward in time, little by little.

(In my first attempt to use a microfilm reader, I dropped the thick roll of film, which swiftly unraveled across the floor of the library, while I frantically scrambled after it in the dark on my hands and knees, climbing over people's ankles and knocking over briefcases and purses. Also, I did not know that you could swivel the film holder to show the writing right-side up, so I spent four hours with my head twisted painfully to one side, trying to read sideways writing. It was excruciating.

(Your first attempt at research will probably not be

as humiliating or as painful as mine was, but you never know. It might be even worse.)

2.

Thou shalt never leap back a couple of generations just because it sound-eth like fun.

Get each generation solidly researched before moving back to the one before it. This goes along with the First Commandment. Think of it as 1-B.

3.

Thou shalt take a class, yea verily, and thus shalt thou learn from experts.

Here are some options to consider:

Local classes

Free classes are offered by many local genealogical societies and/or research libraries and also sometimes by municipal public libraries. Local colleges also sometimes offer night or weekend classes for a small fee.

Correspondence lessons

An excellent class that you can take by mail is offered by the National Genealogical Society. It's called, "American Genealogy: A Basic Course." This allows you to study with some of the best people in the field, and you can complete your assignments at home at your own pace. It also provides you with reference materials and research forms that you will use for years. It costs money, but it's well worth it.

For more information, write to:
> NGS Education Department
> 4527 17th Street, North
> Arlington, VA 22207-2399

Information about the course is also available online at *http://www.ngsgenealogy.org/eduhsc.htm.*

Online courses

Online classes are available from various sources. Brigham Young University offers excellent family history courses over the Internet, and some of their introductory courses are free. (What a wonderful word!) BYU also offers advanced courses that require tuition.

You can check it all out at *http://ce.byu.edu/is/site/index.dhtm.* Choose the "Personal Enrichment" course catalog.

Online Research Guides

A terrific research guide is available at *http://www.rootsweb.com/.* Bookmark this superb Web site; it has a ton of good material for genealogists, and it's free. There's that magic word again.

Family History Library/Centers

The Mormon church promotes family history research through its big Family History Library in Salt Lake City and its smaller Family History Centers (FHCs), which are located in cities all over the world. The Family History Library has a Web site at *http://www.familysearch.org/Eng/Library/FHL/frameset_library.asp* and it has links to a number of educational resources. Click on "Education" on the home page.

Local FHCs sometimes offer free classes, both intro-ductory and advanced. Call (800) 346-6044 to find your nearest FHC. The Family History Library Web page also has a search feature for locating the centers. It's at *http://www.familysearch.org/Eng/Library/FHC/frameset _fhc.asp.* You might as well get the phone number and address of your nearest center now, because the FHC is probably where you'll do a lot of your research. The cen-ters are free public facilities, they are open to the public and they are used gratefully by genealogists of all reli-gious persuasions.

Conventions and seminars

Many genealogical associations sponsor periodic one-, two- or three-day conventions or seminars with lots of classes for beginners and advanced researchers, plus exhibit halls full of vendors. Once again, the Family History Library Web page is a resource to remember: It lists upcoming national conventions and seminars, with dates, locations and contact information.

These gatherings charge an entry fee, but once regis-tered, you can usually attend as many classes as you like. You'll have a wonderful time at one of these big "do's," and you'll learn a lot. Take along a credit card. If you're like me, you'll come home loaded with books and sup-plies that you can't easily find anywhere else.

4.

Join-eth thine local genealogical society, go-eth to meetings and ask-eth questions of the nice people there.

This is how you meet up with other genealogists in

your area, who are the people who will really show you the ropes. You will find that genealogists are generally the most amiable people in the world, when we're not muttering curses and crawling around on our hands and knees, knocking over your briefcase. It is common for researchers to help each other (within reason), and most people will be glad to answer your questions (within reason).

But when you're at a research facility or library, do be considerate of people's concentration and limited research time. Try to ask questions first of the people who seem to be there for that purpose, such as librarians, instructors, research assistants or receptionists.

5.

Thou shalt keep a research log.

Forgive me, fellow researchers, for I have sinned and wasted many hours having to redo research to figure out where I got a piece of information, because my so-called research logs were hit-or-miss.

They'll tell you all about research logs in whatever class you enroll in. Take notes.

6.

Thou shalt cite thy sources
or blush in everlasting chagrin.

You'll be informed of the proper methods for citing sources in the class you take. Take this commandment to heart. This "paperwork" stuff really matters. It's not just people being picky – it allows you (and others) to follow the paper trail of your research, and it is essential to serious research. You might as well develop good habits from the get-go, unlike me.

7.

Thou shalt not accept any information uncritically just because you find it in books or on the Internet.

Treat all information you come across on personal Web sites or in published genealogies as "possibilities"– not as the gospel truth just because it's been published.

You will need to independently verify all information that you incorporate into your own research. The way you'll do that is by personally examining and evaluating the original documents that the information came from (or examining microfilm copies or other facsimiles of the original documents). This is why researchers need to cite their sources – so that others may follow the research trail. It's a red flag if there are no sources listed for the information in a family tree.

Genealogists need to be like tough-minded investigative reporters – skeptical of unsubstantiated claims, and willing to double-check every piece of information via as many independent sources as possible. Also, remember – there's no hurry to get all this done. Your ancestors aren't going anywhere.

8.

Thou shalt regard all family legends with the same skepticism as in the Seventh Commandment.

Don't get locked into a belief in family stories, even if they've been repeated for generations by your most trustworthy relatives. There may be a grain of truth to them – they may even be completely accurate – but they may also be (gasp!) not true. Even the most upstanding ancestor may have mis-remembered or misheard something and, in all good faith, passed it along to the next generation.

I can't tell you how much time I spent researching a certain prime minister to whom (it turned out) my family has no connection whatsoever, except that, like him, we are primates.

9.

**Thou shalt respect the privacy
of all living persons, and
publish nothing concerning
others without their permission.**

And even then, don't.

10.

**Thou shalt treat research facilities,
materials and tools with care,
knowing that thousands of
future researchers will need to use
these very same facilities,
materials and tools after you,
and one of them might be me.**

Do not highlight, underline, rip pages out or dog-ear documents or library books, and don't steal things (amazing that it's necessary to say this, isn't it?). Rewind your microfilm spools and replace material where you found it, unless the library specifically asks that you not re-shelve or refile material.

11.

Thou shalt bookmark the following Web site: *http://www.cyndislist.com*

Cyndi's List has links to almost every genealogy Web site extant, and it's magnificently well organized and updated frequently. The last time I looked, she had almost 154,000 links to genealogy sites. There were 56 links just to "education." (See the Third Commandment.) And it's free.

Browse through Cyndi's List, and see what's available for the areas you are interested in researching (states, towns, countries, etc.) and also see what's out there concerning your ancestors' ethnicities and religion(s). There is so much stuff online, you may feel overwhelmed. That's why you need to take classes and attend seminars: They will show you how to focus your efforts, and how to evaluate sources of information.

Besides the Family History Library, Rootsweb and Cyndi's List, other particularly useful free Web pages are the U.S. National Archives and Records Administration (*http://www.nara.gov*) and the National Genealogical Society (*http://www.ngsgenealogy.org/*).

There are also lots of valuable Web sites that cost money, and many genealogists find them a great resource. Ancestry.com is one of them. You can locate it and others with a search engine, such as *http://www. google.com*.

12.

Be nice to thine ancestors
and they'll be nice to thee.

You'll have to trust me on this one, but put flowers on their graves. Honor them in your heart. There's a saying: "When you drink the water, remember who dug the well." Your ancestors are why you're here today and why your life is as good as it is. Even if you're having a lousy day or a rotten life, it's probably better than most of theirs were.

I notice that this list came out to twelve, not ten. Sorry, I was on a roll.

But Seriously, Folks . . .

What Kind of Ancestor Will You Be?

Occasionally, when I cuss and fuss while searching through illegible old documents, I stop and thank my lucky stars that at least I'm not having to search for late-20th or early-21st century ancestors.

Imagine a century from now trying to locate ancestors who lived in New York City, L.A., London, Tokyo, Mexico City or New Delhi in the year 2000. Especially if they had a fairly common name, an unlisted phone number and no criminal record. And you didn't know their address.

Of course, hard as that would be, locating an ancestor in time and space is the easy part.

It's the real people behind the names and dates that most of us care about. That's why we get into genealogy in the first place – to learn who our ancestors were as people, and to discover and understand the events of their lives. And, unfortunately, that's the hard part – teasing out our ancestors' personalities and life experiences from all-too-brief official records. We treasure every scrap of their writing, every letter we are lucky enough to come across. And to find a diary! Wow, talk about hitting the jackpot.

Which brings us to *us*.

What kinds of records are we leaving for future generations that reveal our own lives, and the lives of the relatives and neighbors we have known? What kind of clues are we leaving behind to help future researchers locate and understand our contemporary families?

Are we going to be the kind of ancestors we wish we'd had?

Today's Records May Be Short-Lived

We sometimes think that the genealogists of the future will have it made, because it feels like our own lives are so well documented, what with photographs and videotapes and all the forms and questionnaires we fill out regularly.

But what good will any of these records do if they're lost, or not available to researchers, or not readable by the computers of the future? What about today's poorly processed photographs that are fading faster than the suntans they record? And our videos that become incompatible with newer technology within a decade? I think future researchers will need at least as much savvy, hard work and good luck to locate their ancestors (that's us) on this crowded planet as we need now to research the past.

And public records are being lost just as relentlessly as records were in the past, too. One example is the U.S. Army personnel records from 1912 to 1963 that were destroyed in a devastating 1973 fire at the National Personnel Records Center. If you or a loved one fought in the U.S. Army in World War I, World War II or Korea, make sure you record as many details of that service as you can. The amount of "official" government information that is available to researchers about that service is quite limited.

Some of the ancestors we are researching today kept their own family records – in Bibles, diaries, journals and correspondence. These kinds of personal testaments are invaluable to family historians. They will be in the future, too. The problem is, our generation has gotten out of the habit of writing letters and keeping diaries. As for "the old family Bible," forget it.

Start writing!

If you don't already keep a diary or journal, the biggest favor you can do for your extended-family's descendants is to record what you know of your recent family history, and your recollections of your relatives – and I don't mean just listing names and dates. We need to "tell the stories" of the events in their lives.

It doesn't have to be great prose; we're not talking Shakespeare here. It just has to be a written record – some kind of notebook or file, printed or handwritten, it doesn't matter – that is kept with your genealogy materials or other important documents.

Recording the history of the generations of the family that you have direct knowledge of will be more important to future generations than any of the research you are doing into the past. Anyone can research the past, but your firsthand knowledge is irreplaceable. You can provide glimpses of your relatives and family life that will never be obtained from any other source.

And don't forget your own connection to the great events of the times. Do you remember the end of World War II? How did you feel? Where were you when you learned what was happening on Sept. 11? What were your reactions? Have you lived through a tornado, a hurricane or an earthquake? What was it like?

Even a few short notes about your experiences and your relatives (and your neighbors) – the ones you knew as a child who have passed on as well as the ones still living – can be invaluable to their descendants. I urge you, of course, to be kind in your recollections, because the notes you leave behind may be all that is ever known about the people you mention. Don't let them be remembered only for the dumbest thing they ever did, or for their worst personality trait. Be accurate, of course, but be fair.

Most of us hate to write. That's because we don't do much of it any more – the telephone took the place of the letter writing that was our ancestors' main mode of communication with those at a distance. So, except for thank you notes or business memos, most of the writing we've done has been in school, where we were graded on our ability to follow rules that felt unrelated to the natural way we talked and thought.

That's one reason people freeze up ("writers block") when faced with a word processor or a paper and pencil. It feels like every word is being dragged out of us under duress. When we do finally get something down on paper, we read it over wincing and groaning, knowing that Miss Whosiwhats in junior high would probably give us a "D."

But as anyone who has read a letter or diary from the 19th century knows, our ancestors had no such inhibitions. Most of our ancestors thought themselves lucky to read and write at all. They didn't worry too much about the niceties. Andrew Jackson spoke for many in that century when he said, "It's a mighty poor mind that can only think of one way to spell a word."

The best writing advice I've ever heard is: "Lower your standards!" Nobody's grading you now, so don't judge yourself so harshly. Relax. Just be yourself, write the way you talk and let 'er rip. It's what you have to say that's important, not how you say it.

Make It Easy on Yourself

Sitting down to write out "everything you can remember about your family" is a daunting prospect. It's like trying to download the entire contents of your brain. But there are ways to make it a lot easier.

I'm making progress in my own "memoirs" by scheduling just five minutes each morning for the task. I started with my grandparents, and wrote everything I could remember about them, then I moved on to my parents. I'm going more or less in chronological order, including things they told me about their childhoods, then progressing on to their educations, marriage, health problems, their friends, where they were living and when, etc.

I try to put in physical details, too, and details about their hobbies and all the family jokes and sayings. Of course, I try to include all the important events, triumphs and disappointments in their lives. I've been surprised at how much I know that I didn't know I knew, how easily the stories unfold and how much you can accomplish if you just keep at it a little at a time.

The writing usually goes on a little longer than five minutes, but rarely longer than fifteen minutes at a time. The format and structure isn't important. Neither is making it "complete." Neatness doesn't count, either. The only thing that counts is getting it done.

I know other family historians who have systems that work equally well for them. One friend, for example, keeps a loose-leaf notebook with dividers for each family member or group, and she jots down notes as she thinks of them. Other, more organized, people might use outlines. One person I know has a goal of writing three paragraphs a day. The important thing is to find something that works for you and to get going and keep going. If you use a computer, print your notes out and keep them with your research. Don't let them languish and be forgotten or lost in your hard drive!

* * * * * * * * *

I wish all family historians would think as much about the future as we do about the past.

Making a record of the people and events we have known in our own generation is where we should start in family history, not where we should end, when we can't think of anything else to research. It's our first obligation, as family historians.

Please remember to be yourself as you write. Don't worry about polishing your prose: You'll only end up sounding stilted and academic. Let your own voice and spirit shine through.

Be the kind of ancestor you wish you'd had. As a family historian, this is the most important legacy you can leave.

LOIS JESEK

Meet the author...
BETH MALTBIE UYEHARA

Beth was a copy editor and writer at
the Los Angeles Times for a number of
years, first in the Times Syndicate,
then in the Special Advertising
Sections department. Before that, she
was an editor and columnist at other
Los Angeles-area newspapers. She was
featured in the PBS series "Ancestors,"
and her story was included in the
series' companion book, "In Search of
Our Ancestors." Beth won the 2000
International Society of Family History
Writers and Editors writer's contest;
her "case-study" entry appeared in
"Ancestry" magazine. Her "Worm's
Eye View" columns, many of which
were written for the "Missing Links"
electronic genealogy newsletter, have
been reprinted in genealogy magazines
throughout the U.S., and in
Australia and Great Britain.
buye@aol.com

...and the illustrator
LOIS JESEK AND K.C. *(KUTE CAT)*

Lois is an art director in the Los Angeles
Times Advertising/Special Sections
Department, where a friendship began and
talents merged to produce a fun book on
a serious subject, genealogy.

After graduation from the Art Center
College of Design, Pasadena, she and her
husband established a successful design
studio in Los Angeles. After two children,
she joined the Times and has been responsible for ads, media kits, books, brochures
and sales presentations, as well as the
Times-Mirror 1984 Olympics. She was
involved with the introduction of Macintosh
computers in all levels of printing and
design and created the digital production
guides that are standards for the industry.

She continues to design and create with
her husband and her fancy cats.
jesek@earthlink.net

Visit
HERITAGE BOOKS, INC.
online at

www.heritagebooks.com

EXTENSIVE SELECTION OF
BOOKS & CD-ROMS
• • •
HISTORY • GENEALOGY • AMERICANA